Christian Worship

New Service Settings

Authorized by the

Commission on Worship of the

Wisconsin Evangelical Lutheran Synod

NORTHWESTERN PUBLISHING HOUSE
Milwaukee, Wisconsin

Copyright © 2002 by Northwestern Publishing House

All rights reserved. No part of this book may be reproduced in any manner whatsoever without prior written permission from the publisher or from the other copyright holders. For further copyright information, see Acknowledgments on pages 72 and 73.

Manufactured in the United States of America.

CONTENTS

	Page
Foreword	4
The Common Service	6
Morning Praise	22
Prayer at the Close of Day I	35
Prayer at the Close of Day II	48
Psalm Index	60
Psalms	61
Psalm Prayers	70
Acknowledgments	72

FOREWORD

The enduring spiritual value of Christian worship comes from its texts—lessons, prayers, creeds, canticles, and hymns—for in these texts is the Word of God. In some cases the texts quote Holy Scripture directly; in others they contain words and phrases the church has carefully crafted to confess the truths of Holy Scripture. Where the Word of God is, there the Holy Spirit operates with his chosen means to regenerate and renew.

Because of its texts, Christian worship has value even without music. The history of the church is filled with examples of believers who gathered around Word and sacrament without music and song during times of persecution, on the battlefield, or because of poverty. Without a note or a chord, these Christians repeated the texts of worship they knew by heart and, as the Spirit worked through the Word, they found comfort, courage, and strength.

Even though Christian worship can occur without music, the church has not removed music from worship. Imitating public worship in their temple and synagogues, the first Christians sang the psalms and canticles of the Old Testament. Later the church began to sing the songs of Mary (*"Magnificat"*), Zechariah (*"Benedictus"*), and the Christmas angels (*"Gloria in Excelsis"*). Hundreds of original hymns and canticles in Greek and Latin followed. We know very little about the sound and style of the music that accompanied these texts, but we do know what believers considered the purpose of these songs to be. Saint Paul wrote to the Christians in Colosse: "Let the word of Christ dwell in you richly . . . as you sing psalms, hymns and spiritual songs with gratitude in your hearts to God" (Colossians 3:16).

Martin Luther loved the Bible; he also loved music. "After theology, I give it the highest praise," he wrote. Luther saw music as a gift of God that, when joined to the Word of God, became the *viva vox evangelii*—the living voice of the gospel. Observing the Creator's power in music and the Spirit's power in the gospel, Luther wrote:

> Thus it was not without reason that the fathers and prophets wanted nothing else to be associated as closely with the Word of God as music. Therefore, we have so many hymns and psalms where message and music join to move the listener's soul. (LW, Vol. 53, p. 323)

The church of the 21st century follows the practice of believers throughout the ages when it places high value on music in public worship. As sermons clarify and explain the Savior's message of grace, so music burrows the message deep into the human heart.

Christian Worship: New Service Settings offers musical settings for three Christian orders of service. Two of them are well known to us. The **Common Service** is a version of the historic Christian liturgy that has served believers for centuries as they have gathered around Word and sacrament. **Morning Praise** (Matins) comes from a set of services used for worship in the academic community. Known as the daily office (*officium* is a Latin word meaning "service"), this set of prayer services also includes Evening Prayer (Vespers) and the third order of service in this collection, **Prayer at the Close of Day** (Compline). While new to us, Prayer at the Close of Day is not new to the church. Christians living in two millennia have used both the liturgy and the services of the daily office to remember in public worship the great things God has done.

What is new about these services is not their texts but their music. Many are familiar with the English chant music that accompanies the Common Service and Morning Praise in *Christian Worship* and *The Lutheran Hymnal*. However, the great texts of these services can be sung to many other musical styles appropriate for worship. In an effort to promote the great texts of the liturgy and the office for worship in our time, the Commission on Worship has authorized the publication of these new services.

Some have claimed—the church father Augustine and the reformer John Calvin are among them—that music detracts from Christian worship because it draws the believer's attention away from the central Word. This is also a concern in today's church as it feels the influence of a musical perspective born in charismatic churches. While this concern does not deter us from adding music to worship, it does make us wary of some musical forms born in the charismatic movement. With these new services, the Commission on Worship seeks to follow the example of believers who have gone before us and to offer musical settings that let the Word be the Spirit's unique means to enliven and empower.

James P. Tiefel
March 2002

THE COMMON SERVICE

HYMN

STAND

M In the name of the Father and of the Son and of the Holy Spirit.

C **Amen.**

CONFESSION OF SINS

M Beloved in the Lord: let us draw near with a true heart and confess our sins to God our Father, asking him in the name of our Lord Jesus Christ to grant us forgiveness.

The congregation may kneel.

C **Holy and merciful Father, I confess that I am by nature sinful and that I have disobeyed you in my thoughts, words, and actions. I have done what is evil and failed to do what is good. For this I deserve your punishment both now and in eternity. But I am truly sorry for my sins, and trusting in my Savior Jesus Christ, I pray: Lord, have mercy on me, a sinner.**

LORD, HAVE MERCY

Kyrie

C Lord, have mercy on us. Christ, have mercy on us. Lord, have mercy on us. Amen.

M God, our heavenly Father, has been merciful to us and has given his only Son to be the atoning sacrifice for our sins. Therefore, as a called servant of Christ and by his authority, I forgive you all your sins in the name of the Father and of the Son ✠ and of the Holy Spirit.

C **Amen.**

The service continues on page 8 with PRAYER AND PRAISE.

THE COMMON SERVICE

(Alternate Beginning)

HYMN

STAND

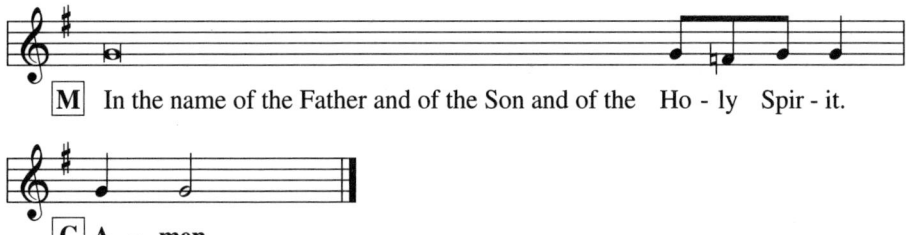

M In the name of the Father and of the Son and of the Holy Spirit.

C A - men.

CONFESSION OF SINS

M Beloved in the Lord: let us draw near with a true heart and confess our sins to God our Father, asking him in the name of our Lord Jesus Christ to grant us forgiveness.

The congregation may kneel.

C **Holy and merciful Father, I confess that I am by nature sinful and that I have disobeyed you in my thoughts, words, and actions.**

Lord, have mer - cy on us.

COMMON SERVICE

C I have done what is evil and failed to do what is good. For this I deserve your punishment both now and in eternity.

Christ, have mer-cy on us.

C But I am truly sorry for my sins, and trusting in my Savior Jesus Christ, I pray: Lord, have mercy on me, a sinner.

Lord, have mer-cy on us. A-men.

M God, our heavenly Father, has been merciful to us and has given his only Son to be the atoning sacrifice for our sins. Therefore, as a called servant of Christ and by his authority, I forgive you all your sins in the name of the Father and of the Son ✠ and of the Holy Spirit.

C Amen.

PRAYER AND PRAISE

M In the peace of forgiveness, let us praise the Lord.

GLORY TO GOD or another song of praise is sung.

GLORY TO GOD
Gloria in Excelsis

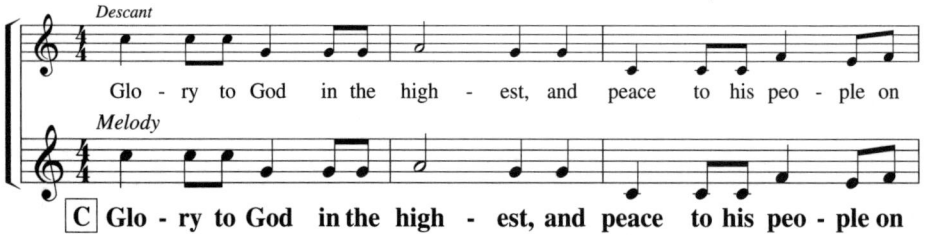

Descant
Glo-ry to God in the high - est, and peace to his peo-ple on
Melody
C Glo-ry to God in the high - est, and peace to his peo-ple on

8

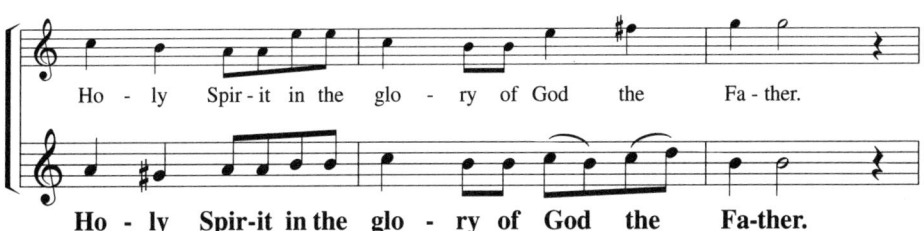

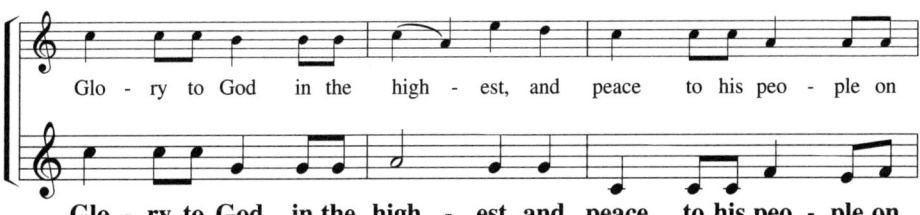

PRAYER OF THE DAY

M The Lord be with you.

C And also with you.

M Let us pray.

The minister says the Prayer of the Day.

C Amen.

BE SEATED

THE WORD

FIRST LESSON

PSALM OF THE DAY

SECOND LESSON

VERSE OF THE DAY

The choir sings the proper VERSE OF THE DAY, or the minister speaks the Verse.

STAND

GOSPEL

After the announcement of the Gospel, the congregation sings:

C Glo-ry be to you, O Lord! Glo-ry be to you, O Lord!

After the Gospel, the congregation sings:

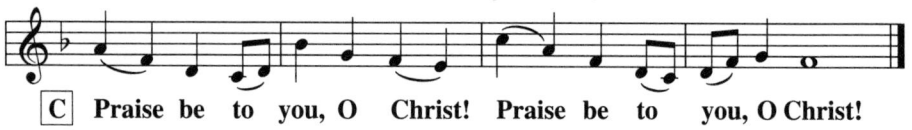

C Praise be to you, O Christ! Praise be to you, O Christ!

NICENE CREED

> We believe in one God, the Father, the Almighty,
>> maker of heaven and earth,
>> of all that is,
>> seen and unseen.
>
> We believe in one Lord, Jesus Christ, the only Son of God,
>> eternally begotten of the Father,
>> God from God, Light from Light, true God from true God,
>> begotten, not made,
>> of one being with the Father.
> Through him all things were made.
> For us and for our salvation, he came down from heaven,
>> was incarnate of the Holy Spirit and the virgin Mary,
>> and became fully human.
> For our sake he was crucified under Pontius Pilate.

He suffered death and was buried.
On the third day he rose again in accordance with the Scriptures.
He ascended into heaven
    and is seated at the right hand of the Father.
He will come again in glory to judge the living and the dead,
    and his kingdom will have no end.

We believe in the Holy Spirit,
    the Lord, the giver of life,
    who proceeds from the Father and the Son,
    who in unity with the Father and the Son is worshiped and glorified,
    who has spoken through the prophets.
We believe in one holy Christian and apostolic Church.
We acknowledge one baptism for the forgiveness of sins.
We look for the resurrection of the dead
    and the life of the world to come. Amen.

OR

APOSTLES' CREED

I believe in God, the Father almighty,
    maker of heaven and earth.

I believe in Jesus Christ, his only Son, our Lord,
    who was conceived by the Holy Spirit,
    born of the virgin Mary,
    suffered under Pontius Pilate,
    was crucified, died, and was buried.
He descended into hell.
The third day he rose again from the dead.
He ascended into heaven
    and is seated at the right hand of God the Father almighty.
From there he will come to judge the living and the dead.

I believe in the Holy Spirit,
    the holy Christian Church,
        the communion of saints,
    the forgiveness of sins,
    the resurrection of the body,
    and the life everlasting. Amen.

BE SEATED

COMMON SERVICE

HYMN OF THE DAY

SERMON

STAND

After the sermon, the congregation sings:

C Create in me a pure heart, O God, and renew a right spirit within me. Do not cast me away from your presence or take your Holy Spirit from me. Restore to me the joy of your salvation, and uphold, uphold me with your free Spirit.

BE SEATED

OFFERING

STAND

PRAYER OF THE CHURCH

LORD'S PRAYER

| **C** Our Father in heaven, | OR | Our Father, who art in heaven, |

C Our Father in heaven,   OR   Our Father, who art in heaven,
    hallowed be your name,   hallowed be thy name,
    your kingdom come,   thy kingdom come,
    your will be done   thy will be done
        on earth as in heaven.   on earth as it is in heaven.
Give us today our daily bread.   Give us this day our daily bread;
Forgive us our sins,   and forgive us our trespasses,
    as we forgive those   as we forgive those
    who sin against us.   who trespass against us;
Lead us not into temptation,   and lead us not into temptation,
but deliver us from evil.   but deliver us from evil.
For the kingdom, the power,   For thine is the kingdom
    and the glory are yours   and the power and the glory
    now and forever. Amen.   forever and ever. Amen.

> **When there is no Communion, the service continues on page 20.**

THE SACRAMENT

PREFACE

M The Lord be with you.

C And also with you.

M Lift up your hearts.

C We lift them up to the Lord.

M Let us give thanks to the Lord, our God.

C It is good and right so to do.

M It is truly good and right that we should at all times and in all places give you thanks, O Lord, holy Father, almighty and everlasting God, through Jesus Christ, our Lord,

PROPER PREFACES

Advent: whose way John the Baptist prepared when he called people to repentance and pointed to Jesus as the Lamb of God who takes away the sin of the world. (Therefore . . .)

Christmas: for in the wonder and mystery of his birth you have opened our eyes to the glory of your grace and renewed in our hearts the fervor of your love. (Therefore . . .)

Epiphany: who lived among us as a human being and revealed his glory as your only Son, full of grace and truth. (Therefore . . .)

Lent: who brought the gift of salvation to all people by his death on the tree of the cross, so that the devil, who overcame us by a tree would in turn by a tree be overcome. (Therefore . . .)

Easter/Ascension: and we praise you especially for the glorious resurrection of your Son, the true Passover Lamb, who by his sacrifice took away the sins of the world and by his resurrection restored everlasting life. (Therefore . . .)

Pentecost: who on this day kept his promise and poured out the Holy Spirit to empower his Church to proclaim the gospel in all the world. (Therefore . . .)

The Holy Trinity: and now we confess that you, with your Son and the Holy Spirit, are one God and one Lord, and we acknowledge you as our Creator, Redeemer, and Sanctifier. (Therefore . . .)

Sundays after Pentecost: who promised that wherever two or three come together in his name, there he is with them to shepherd his flock till he comes again in glory. (Therefore . . .)

End Time: who preserves his Church to the end of time when he will come again as king to judge all people and take his own to glory. (Therefore . . .)

Minor Festivals: who in blessing his saints of the past has given us glorious assurance and hope that, following their example of faith, we may run with perseverance the race marked out for us, and receive the crown of glory that will never fade away. (Therefore . . .)

Therefore, with all the saints on earth and hosts of heaven, we praise your holy name and join their glorious song:

HOLY, HOLY, HOLY
Sanctus

COMMON SERVICE

WORDS OF INSTITUTION

M Our Lord Jesus Christ, on the night he was betrayed, took bread; and when he had given thanks, he broke it and gave it to his disciples, saying, "Take and eat; this is my body, which is given for you. Do this in remembrance of me."

Then he took the cup, gave thanks, and gave it to them, saying, "Drink from it, all of you; this is my blood of the new covenant, which is poured out for you for the forgiveness of sins. Do this, whenever you drink it, in remembrance of me."

M The peace of the Lord be with you always.

C Amen.

O CHRIST, LAMB OF GOD
Agnus Dei

C: O Christ, Lamb of God, you take away the sin of the world; have mercy on us. O Christ, Lamb of God, you take away the sin of the world; have mercy on us. O Christ, Lamb of God, you take away the

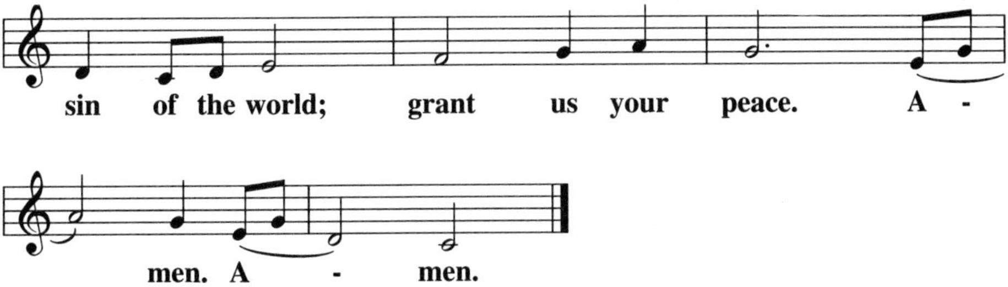

COMMON SERVICE

♪ sin of the world; grant us your peace. A-
men. A - men.

BE SEATED

DISTRIBUTION

During the distribution the congregation may sing one or more hymns.

THANKSGIVING

STAND

The SONG OF SIMEON or a song of thanksgiving is sung.

SONG OF SIMEON
Nunc Dimittis

C In peace, Lord, you let your ser-vant now de-part ac-cord-ing to your word. For my eyes have seen your sal-va-tion, which you have pre-pared for ev-'ry peo-ple, a light to light-en the Gen-tiles and the glo-ry, the glo-ry of your peo-ple Is-ra-el.

COMMON SERVICE

| M | O give thanks to the Lord, for he is good.

| C | **And his mercy endures forever.**

| M | We give thanks, almighty God, that you have refreshed us with this holy supper. We pray that through it you will strengthen our faith in you and increase our love for one another. We ask this in the name of Jesus Christ, our Lord, who lives and reigns with you and the Holy Spirit, one God, now and forever.

OR

O God the Father, source of all goodness, in your loving kindness you sent your Son to share our humanity. We thank you that through him you have given us pardon and peace in this sacrament. We also pray that you will not forsake us but will rule our hearts and minds by your Holy Spirit so that we willingly serve you day after day, through Jesus Christ, our Lord, who lives and reigns with you and the Holy Spirit, one God, now and forever.

| C | **Amen.**

| M | The Lord bless you and keep you.
The Lord make his face shine on you and be gracious to you.
The Lord look on you with favor and ✠ give you peace.

| C | **Amen.**

> **When there is no Communion, the service concludes as follows:**

BE SEATED

HYMN

STAND

| M | Blessed Lord, you have given us your Holy Scriptures for our learning. May we so hear them, read, learn, and take them to heart, that being strengthened and comforted by your holy Word, we may cling to the blessed hope of everlasting life, through Jesus Christ, our Lord, who lives and reigns with you and the Holy Spirit, one God, now and forever.

OR

Almighty God, grant to your Church the Holy Spirit and the wisdom that comes from above. Let nothing hinder your Word from being freely proclaimed to the joy and edifying of Christ's holy people, so that we may serve you in steadfast faith and confess your name as long as we live, through Jesus Christ, our Lord, who lives and reigns with you and the Holy Spirit, one God, now and forever.

C **Amen.**

M The Lord bless you and keep you.
The Lord make his face shine on you and be gracious to you.
The Lord look on you with favor and ✠ give you peace.

C **Amen.**

MORNING PRAISE

MATINS

STAND

OPENING HYMN

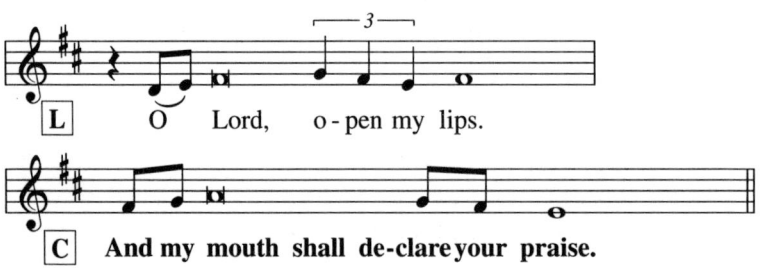

L: O Lord, o-pen my lips.

C: And my mouth shall de-clare your praise.

L: Hasten to save me, O God.

C: O Lord, come quickly to help me.

L: Give glory to God, our light and our life.

C: Come, oh, come, let us wor-ship.

MORNING PRAISE

COME, OH, COME, LET US SING TO THE LORD
Venite

MORNING PRAISE

BE SEATED

PSALM 63

MORNING PRAISE

LESSON

SEASONAL RESPONSE

Following the lesson, the SEASONAL RESPONSE may be sung or said. Music can be found in **CHRISTIAN WORSHIP: ALTAR BOOK** *and* **SEASONAL RESPONSES.**

Advent: The Lord will come again in glory. The Spirit and the Church cry out: Come, Lord Jesus, come.

Christmas/Epiphany: We have seen his glory, the glory of the one and only Son, who came from the Father, full of grace and truth.

Lent: All we like sheep have gone astray, and the Lord has laid on him the iniquity of us all. By his wounds we are healed.

Easter/Ascension: The Lord is risen! He is risen indeed! Alleluia! Death has been swallowed up in victory. Alleluia!

Pentecost: Come, Holy Spirit! Fill the hearts of your faithful people, and kindle in us the fire of your love. Alleluia!

General/Thanksgiving: Give thanks to the Lord; call on his name; make known among the nations what he has done.

HYMN

MORNING PRAISE

The **SERMON** *may follow.*

STAND

SONG OF ZECHARIAH replaces YOU ARE GOD; WE PRAISE YOU during the Advent season.

YOU ARE GOD; WE PRAISE YOU
Te Deum

L *Refrain*

C *Refrain*

You are God; we praise you. You are Lord; we ac-claim you.

To you, O Father holy, all creation offers praise.

Verses

L 1. With the angels in heaven,
2. Creator of all things, **C** We praise you, we
3. O Christ, King of glory,

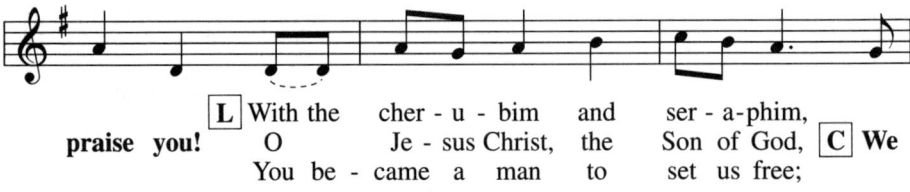

L With the cherubim and seraphim,
praise you! O Jesus Christ, the Son of God, **C** We
You became a man to set us free;

OR

MORNING PRAISE

SONG OF ZECHARIAH
Benedictus

BE SEATED

The OFFERING *may follow.*

STAND

LORD, HAVE MERCY
Kyrie

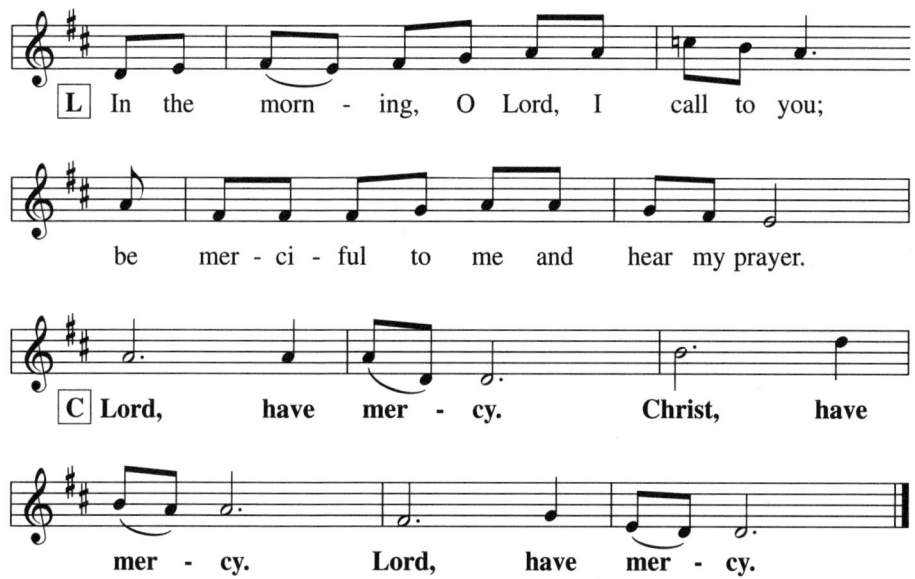

L In the morning, O Lord, I call to you;
be merciful to me and hear my prayer.
C Lord, have mercy. Christ, have mercy. Lord, have mercy.

LORD'S PRAYER

C Our Father in heaven,
    hallowed be your name,
    your kingdom come,
    your will be done
        on earth as in heaven.
Give us today our daily bread.
Forgive us our sins,
    as we forgive those
    who sin against us.
Lead us not into temptation,
but deliver us from evil.
For the kingdom, the power,
    and the glory are yours
    now and forever. Amen.

OR

Our Father, who art in heaven,
    hallowed be thy name,
    thy kingdom come,
    thy will be done
        on earth as it is in heaven.
Give us this day our daily bread;
and forgive us our trespasses,
    as we forgive those
    who trespass against us;
and lead us not into temptation,
but deliver us from evil.
For thine is the kingdom
    and the power and the glory
    forever and ever. Amen.

MORNING PRAISE

The PRAYER OF THE DAY or a prayer for the season or another prayer may follow, concluding with the PRAYER FOR GRACE.

PRAYER FOR GRACE

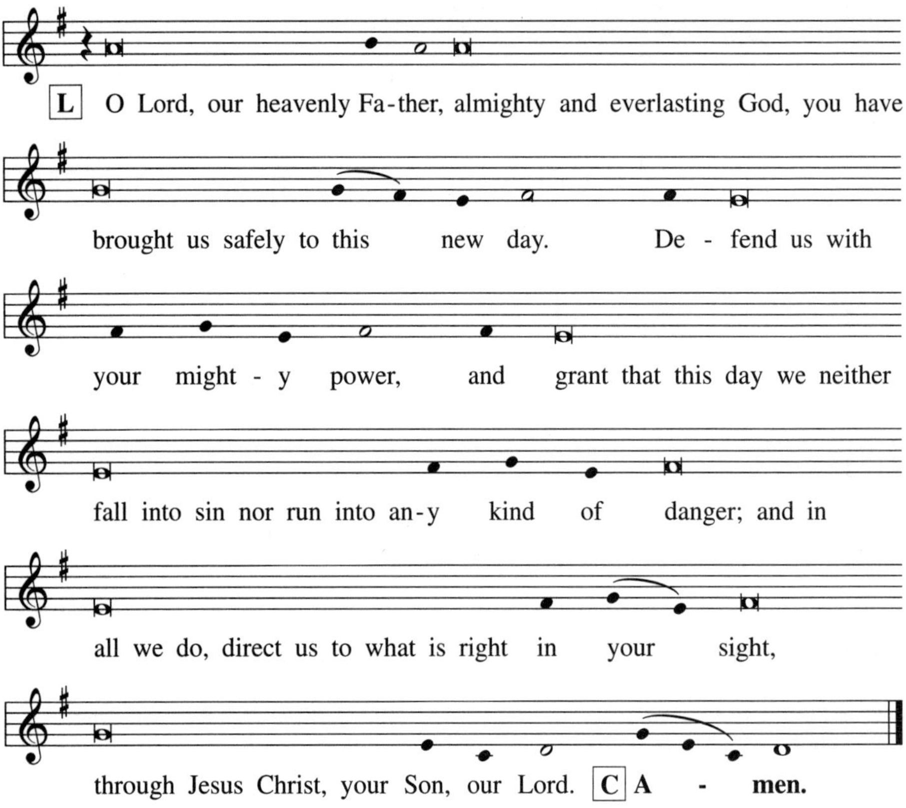

L   O Lord, our heavenly Father, almighty and everlasting God, you have brought us safely to this new day. Defend us with your mighty power, and grant that this day we neither fall into sin nor run into any kind of danger; and in all we do, direct us to what is right in your sight, through Jesus Christ, your Son, our Lord.   C   Amen.

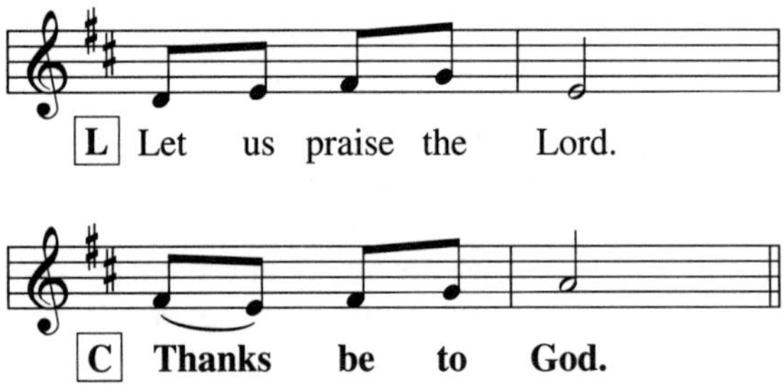

L   Let us praise the Lord.

C   Thanks be to God.

BLESSING

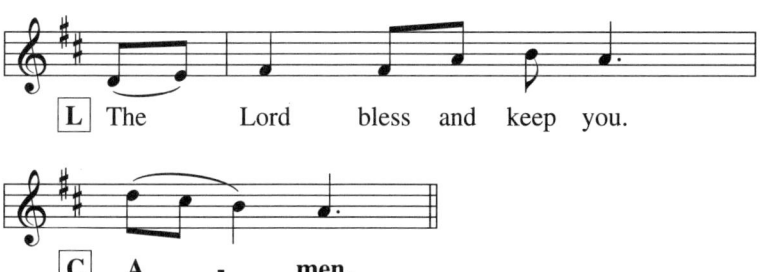

L: The Lord bless and keep you.

C: A - men.

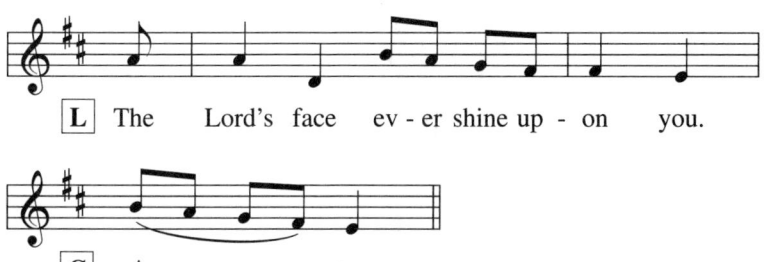

L: The Lord's face ev-er shine up-on you.

C: A - men.

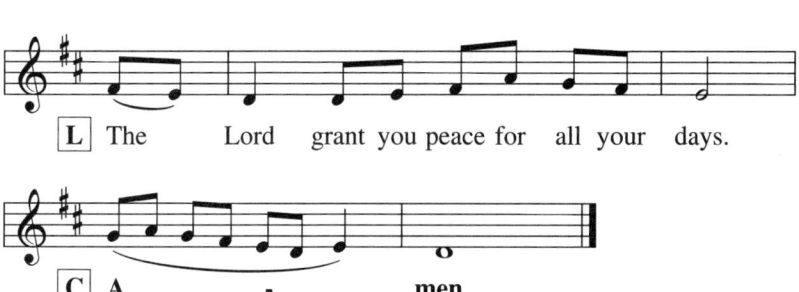

L: The Lord grant you peace for all your days.

C: A - men.

PRAYER AT THE CLOSE OF DAY
COMPLINE: Setting I

"Prayer at the Close of Day" is a version of the historic rite called Compline. It is the final service of the day before one retires for the night. The congregation gathers in silence. Preservice music is omitted and the lighting is subdued. This is a time for prayer and meditation. The believer finds peace in God's forgiveness and security under the shadow of his wings.

REMAIN SEATED

The following sentences are sung or said.

L The Lord Almighty grant us a quiet night and peace at the last.

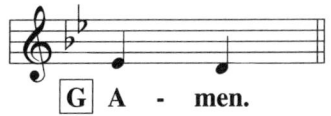
G A - men.

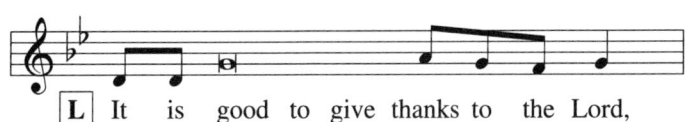
L It is good to give thanks to the Lord,

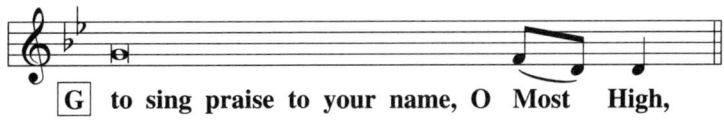
G to sing praise to your name, O Most High,

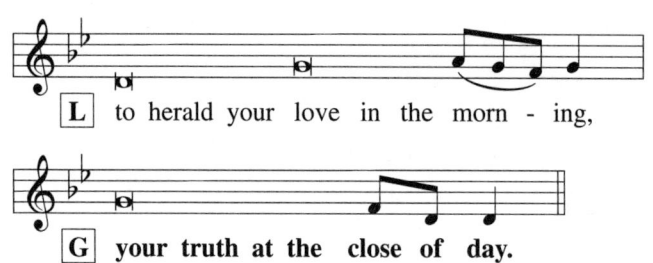

L to herald your love in the morn - ing,

G your truth at the close of day.

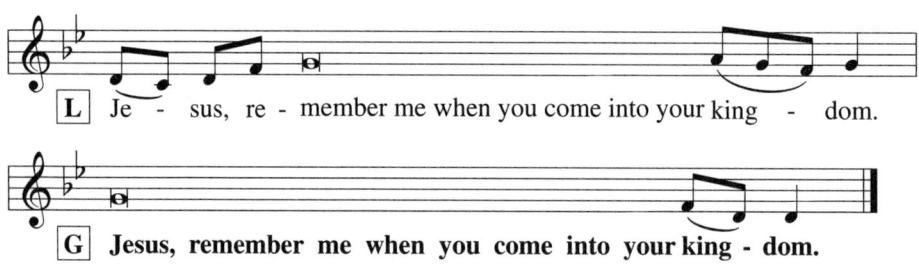

L Je - sus, re - member me when you come into your king - dom.

G Jesus, remember me when you come into your king - dom.

EVENING HYMN

The following or another evening hymn is sung.

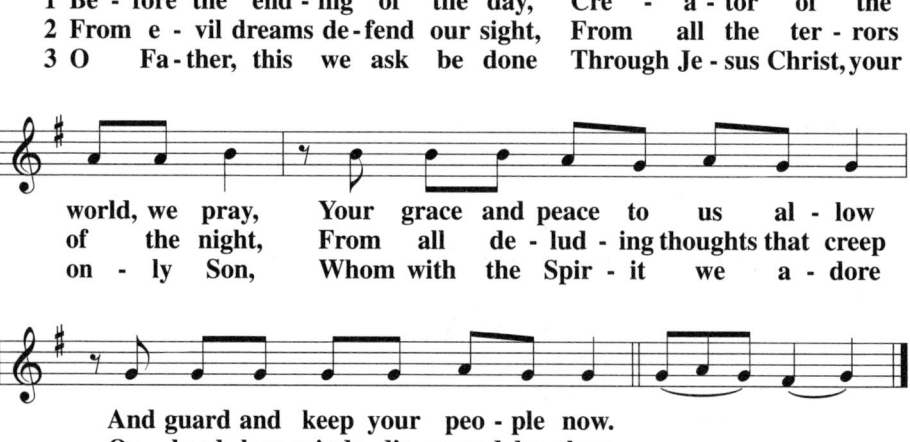

1 Be - fore the end - ing of the day, Cre - a - tor of the world, we pray, Your grace and peace to us al - low And guard and keep your peo - ple now.

2 From e - vil dreams de - fend our sight, From all the ter - rors of the night, From all de - lud - ing thoughts that creep On heed - less minds dis - armed by sleep.

3 O Fa - ther, this we ask be done Through Je - sus Christ, your only Son, Whom with the Spir - it we a - dore For - ev - er and for - ev - er - more. A - men.

The congregation may kneel.

CONFESSION OF SINS

L Our help is in the name of the Lord,

G **who made heaven and earth.**

L Let us confess our sins in the presence of God and of one another.

Silence for self-examination

L I confess to God Almighty, before the whole company of heaven,
      and to you, my brothers and sisters,
  that I have sinned in thought, word, and deed
    by my fault,
    by my own fault,
    by my own grievous fault;
  wherefore I pray God Almighty to have mercy on me,
    forgive me all my sins,
    and bring me to everlasting life.

G **The almighty and merciful Lord grant you pardon, forgiveness, and remission of all your sins.**

L Amen.

G **I confess to God Almighty, before the whole company of heaven,**
      and to you, my brothers and sisters,
  that I have sinned in thought, word, and deed
    by my fault,
    by my own fault,
    by my own grievous fault;
  wherefore I pray God Almighty to have mercy on me,
    forgive me all my sins,
    and bring me to everlasting life.

L The almighty and merciful Lord grant you pardon, forgiveness,
  and remission of all your sins.

G **Amen.**

PRAYER AT THE CLOSE OF DAY I

OR

L Almighty God, our heavenly Father,

G **we have sinned against you
in our thoughts,
in our words,
in our deeds,
and in all that we have not done.
Forgive us in the name of our Lord Jesus Christ.
Deliver and restore us,
that we may rest in peace.**

L By the mercy of God we are redeemed by Jesus Christ,
and in him we are forgiven.
Let us rest in his peace until the rising of the sun
when we shall serve him in newness of life.

G **Amen.**

REMAIN SEATED

PSALM

One or more psalms are sung or said. Psalm 91 is usually first. See pages 61-69.

PSALM 91

Keep me, keep me as the ap-ple of your eye.

Hide me, hide me in the shad-ow of your wings.

Psalm Tone

He who dwells in the shelter of the / Most High
> will rest in the shadow of the Al- / mighty.
>> I will say / of the L<small>ORD</small>,
>>> "He is my refuge and my fortress, my God, in / whom I trust."

Surely he will save you from the / fowler's snare
> and from the deadly / pestilence.
>> He will cover you with his feathers, and under his wings you will find / refuge;
>>> his faithfulness will be your shield and / rampart.

Refrain

You will not fear the terror of night, nor the arrow that / flies by day,
> nor the pestilence that stalks in the darkness, nor the plague that destroys at / midday.
>> A thousand may fall at your side, ten thousand at / your right hand,
>>> but it will not come / near you.

Refrain

If you make the Most High your dwelling—even the L<small>ORD</small>, who is my / refuge—
> then no harm will befall you, no disaster will come / near your tent.
>> For he will command his angels concerning you to guard you in / all your ways;
>>> they will lift you up in their hands, so that you will not strike your foot
>>>> a- / gainst a stone.

Glory be to the Father and / to the Son
> **and to the Holy / Spirit,**
>> **as it was in the be- / ginning,**
>>> **is now, and will be forever. / Amen.**

Refrain

Silence for meditation

L	Lord God, our refuge and fortress, your faithfulness has protected us through this day. Now send your holy angels to guard us from danger through this night. Give us peaceful rest, free from fear, that we may wake refreshed to serve you, through Jesus Christ, your Son, our Lord.

G	**Amen.**

LESSON

One or more of the following or other lessons are read.

The Spirit of the Sovereign LORD is on me, because the LORD has anointed me to preach good news to the poor. He has sent me to bind up the brokenhearted, to proclaim freedom for the captives and release from darkness for the prisoners, to proclaim the year of the LORD's favor and the day of vengeance of our God, to comfort all who mourn, and provide for those who grieve in Zion—to bestow on them a crown of beauty instead of ashes, the oil of gladness instead of mourning, and a garment of praise instead of a spirit of despair. They will be called oaks of righteousness, a planting of the LORD for the display of his splendor (Isaiah 61:1-3).

Although our sins testify against us, O LORD, do something for the sake of your name. For our backsliding is great; we have sinned against you. O Hope of Israel, its Savior in times of distress, why are you like a stranger in the land, like a traveler who stays only a night? Why are you like a man taken by surprise, like a warrior powerless to save? You are among us, O LORD, and we bear your name; do not forsake us! (Jeremiah 14:7-9).

Come to me, all you who are weary and burdened, and I will give you rest. Take my yoke upon you and learn from me, for I am gentle and humble in heart, and you will find rest for your souls. For my yoke is easy and my burden is light (Matthew 11:28-30).

Peace I leave with you; my peace I give you. I do not give to you as the world gives. Do not let your hearts be troubled and do not be afraid (John 14:27).

For I am convinced that neither death nor life, neither angels nor demons, neither the present nor the future, nor any powers, neither height nor depth, nor anything else in all creation, will be able to separate us from the love of God that is in Christ Jesus our Lord (Romans 8:38,39).

May the God of peace, who through the blood of the eternal covenant brought back from the dead our Lord Jesus, that great Shepherd of the sheep, equip you with everything good for doing his will, and may he work in us what is pleasing to him, through Jesus Christ, to whom be glory for ever and ever. Amen (Hebrews 13:20,21).

Humble yourselves, therefore, under God's mighty hand, that he may lift you up in due time. Cast all your anxiety on him because he cares for you. Be self-controlled and alert. Your enemy the devil prowls around like a roaring lion looking for someone to devour. Resist him, standing firm in the faith, because you know that your brothers throughout the world are undergoing the same kind of sufferings (1 Peter 5:6-9).

PRAYER AT THE CLOSE OF DAY I

The following response is sung or said.

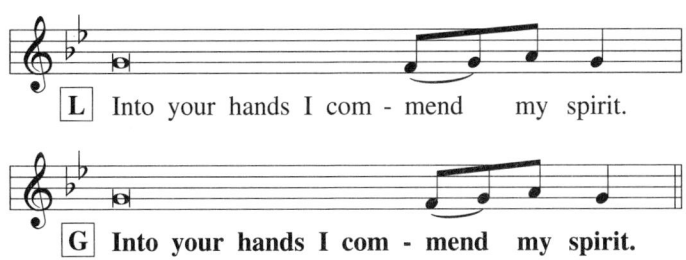

L Into your hands I commend my spirit.

G Into your hands I commend my spirit.

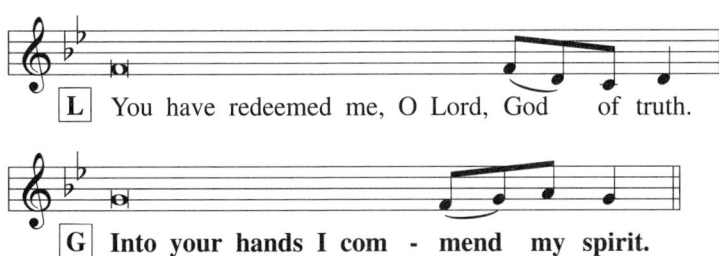

L You have redeemed me, O Lord, God of truth.

G Into your hands I commend my spirit.

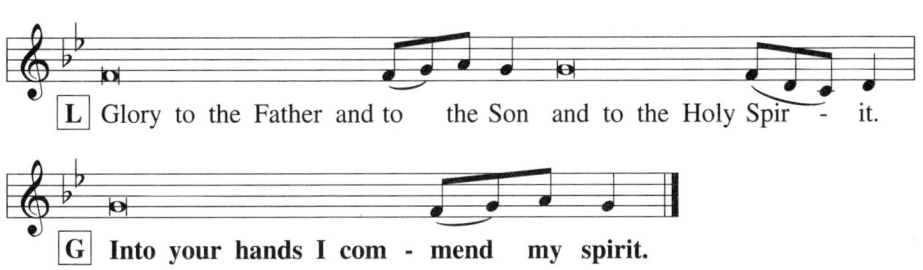

L Glory to the Father and to the Son and to the Holy Spirit.

G Into your hands I commend my spirit.

HYMN

PRAYER

The following are sung or said.

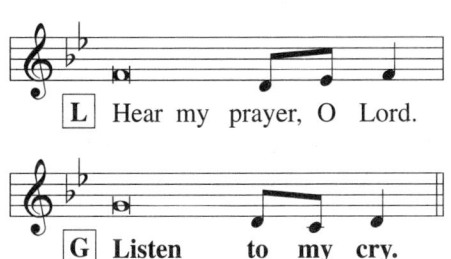

L Hear my prayer, O Lord.

G Listen to my cry.

PRAYER AT THE CLOSE OF DAY I

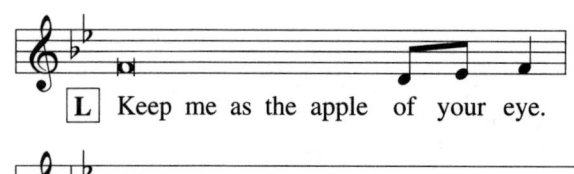

L Keep me as the apple of your eye.

G Hide me in the shadow of your wings.

L In righteousness I shall see you.

G When I awake, your presence will give me joy.

One or more of the following prayers are sung or said.

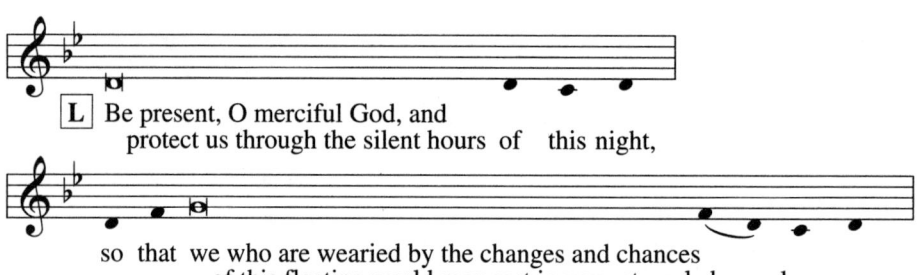

L Be present, O merciful God, and
protect us through the silent hours of this night,
so that we who are wearied by the changes and chances
of this fleeting world may rest in your eternal change-less-ness,
through Jesus Christ our Lord.

G A - men.

OR

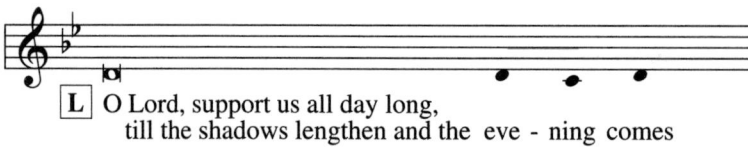

L O Lord, support us all day long,
till the shadows lengthen and the eve - ning comes

PRAYER AT THE CLOSE OF DAY I

OR

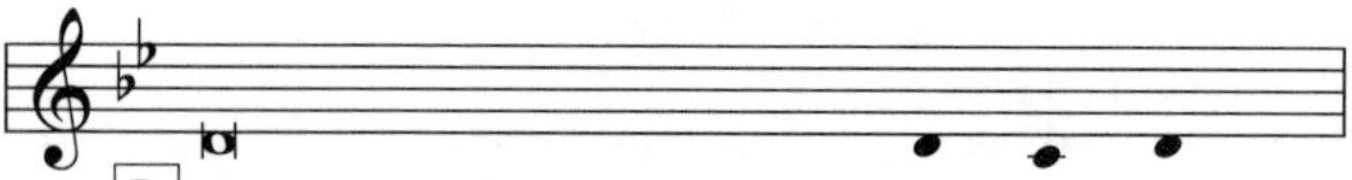

L Keep watch, dear Lord, with those who watch or work or weep this night, and give your angels charge over those who sleep. 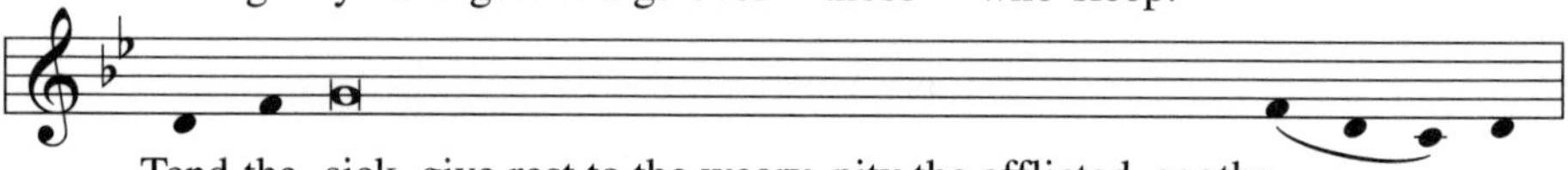 Tend the sick, give rest to the weary, pity the afflicted, soothe the suffering, bless the dying—and all for your love's sake, through Jesus Christ our Lord.

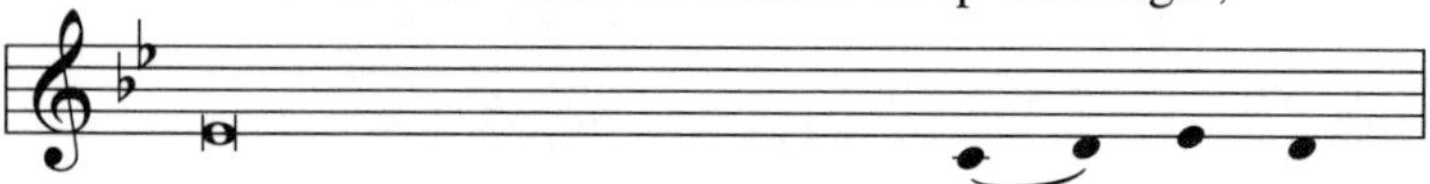

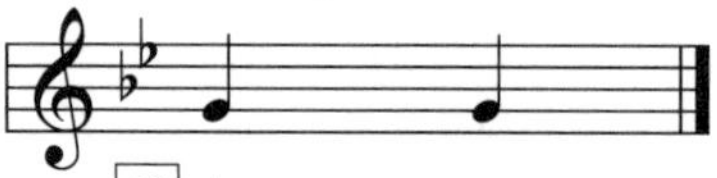

G A - men.

OR

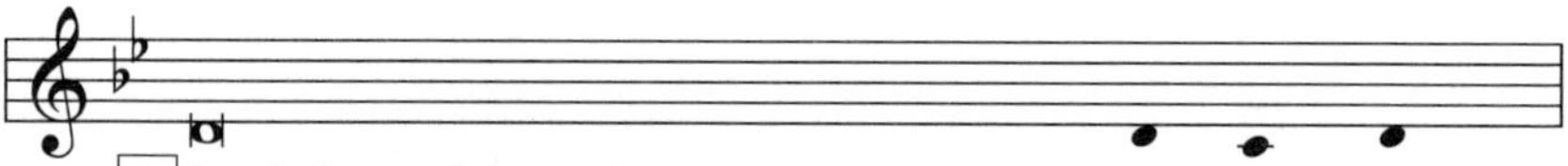

L Look down, O Lord, from your heavenly throne, and illuminate this night with your cel - es - tial brightness, that by night as by day your people may glorify your ho - ly name, through Jesus Christ our Lord.

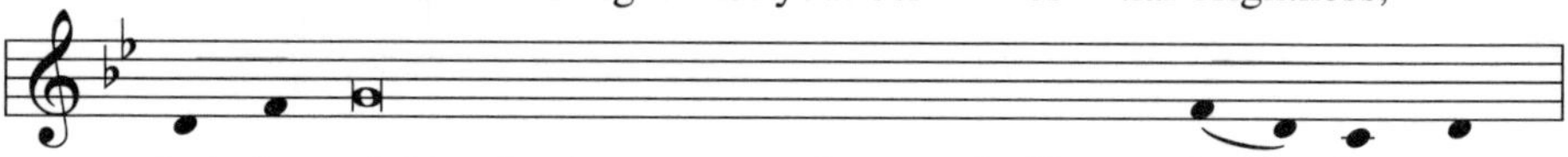

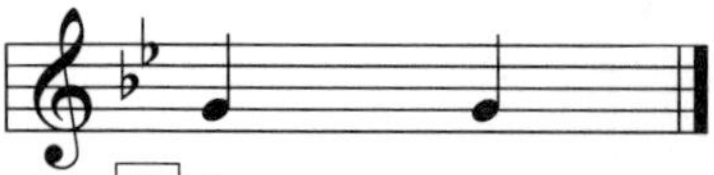

G A - men.

OR for Saturday

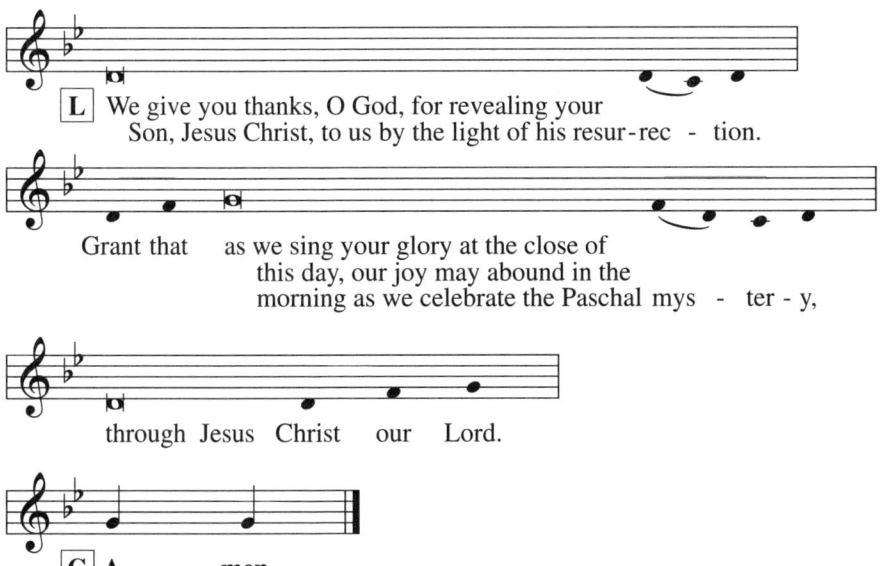

L We give you thanks, O God, for revealing your Son, Jesus Christ, to us by the light of his resurrection. Grant that as we sing your glory at the close of this day, our joy may abound in the morning as we celebrate the Paschal mystery, through Jesus Christ our Lord.

G A - men.

The Lord's Prayer is said or sung on a single tone.

G Our Father in heaven, 　　hallowed be your name, 　　your kingdom come, 　　your will be done 　　　　on earth as in heaven. Give us today our daily bread. Forgive us our sins, 　　as we forgive those 　　who sin against us. Lead us not into temptation, but deliver us from evil. For the kingdom, the power, 　　and the glory are yours 　　now and forever. Amen.	OR　Our Father, who art in heaven, 　　hallowed be thy name, 　　thy kingdom come, 　　thy will be done 　　　　on earth as it is in heaven. Give us this day our daily bread; and forgive us our trespasses, 　　as we forgive those 　　who trespass against us; and lead us not into temptation, but deliver us from evil. For thine is the kingdom 　　and the power and the glory 　　forever and ever. Amen.

HYMN

GOSPEL CANTICLE

The following is sung or said.

Antiphon

L Guide us waking, O Lord,

G and guard us sleeping,

L that awake we may watch with Christ

G and asleep we may rest in peace.

Song of Simeon

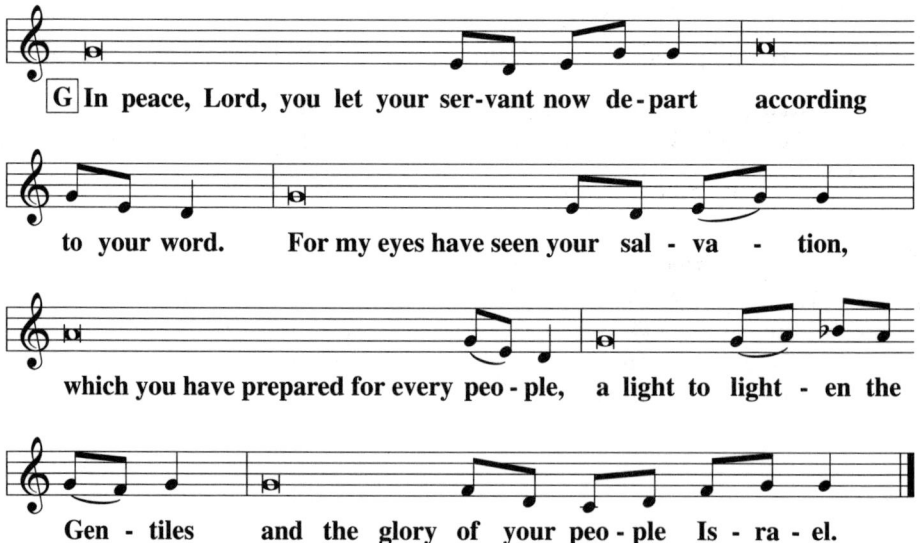

G In peace, Lord, you let your servant now depart according to your word. For my eyes have seen your salvation, which you have prepared for every people, a light to lighten the Gentiles and the glory of your people Israel.

Antiphon

L Guide us waking, O Lord,
G and guard us sleeping,
L that awake we may watch with Christ
G and asleep we may rest in peace.

BLESSING

The Blessing is sung or said.

L The almighty and merciful Lord—the Father, the Son, (✠) and the Holy Spirit—bless us and keep us.
G Amen.

PRAYER AT THE CLOSE OF DAY
COMPLINE: Setting II

"Prayer at the Close of Day" is a version of the historic rite called Compline. It is the final service of the day before one retires for the night. The congregation gathers in silence. Preservice music is omitted, and the lighting is subdued. This is a time for prayer and meditation. The believer finds peace in God's forgiveness and security under the shadow of his wings.

REMAIN SEATED

The following sentences are sung or said.

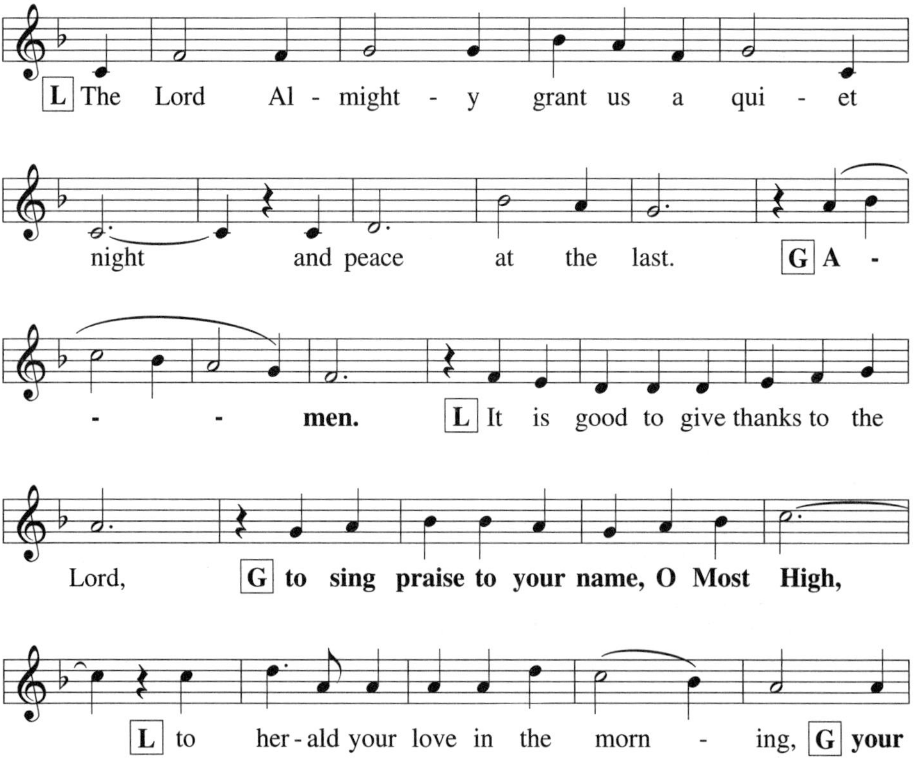

L The Lord Al-might-y grant us a qui-et night and peace at the last. G A- - - men. L It is good to give thanks to the Lord, G to sing praise to your name, O Most High, L to her-ald your love in the morn - ing, G your

EVENING HYMN

The following or another evening hymn is sung.

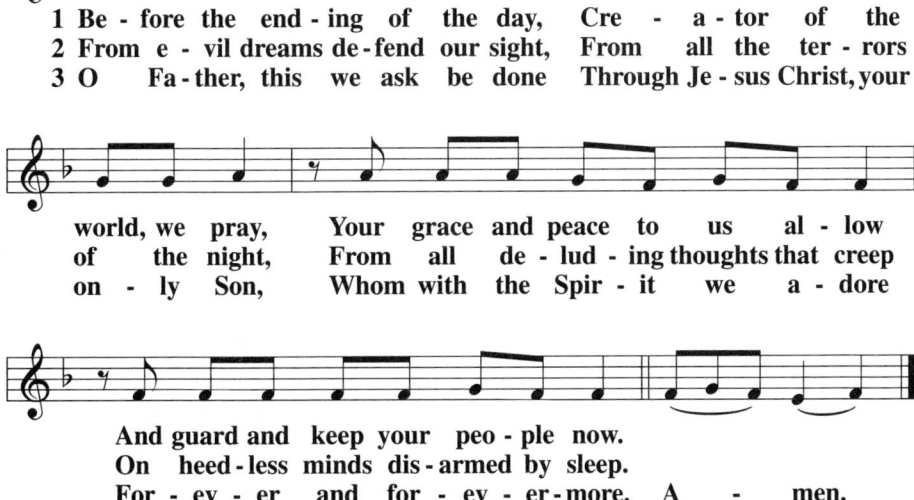

The congregation may kneel.

CONFESSION OF SINS

L Our help is in the name of the Lord,

G **who made heaven and earth.**

L Let us confess our sins in the presence of God and of one another.

Silence for self-examination

L I confess to God Almighty, before the whole company of heaven,
      and to you, my brothers and sisters,
   that I have sinned in thought, word, and deed
      by my fault,
      by my own fault,
      by my own grievous fault;
   wherefore I pray God Almighty to have mercy on me,
      forgive me all my sins,
      and bring me to everlasting life.

G **The almighty and merciful Lord grant you pardon, forgiveness, and remission of all your sins.**

L Amen.

G **I confess to God Almighty, before the whole company of heaven,**
      and to you, my brothers and sisters,
   that I have sinned in thought, word, and deed
      by my fault,
      by my own fault,
      by my own grievous fault;
   wherefore I pray God Almighty to have mercy on me,
      forgive me all my sins,
      and bring me to everlasting life.

L The almighty and merciful Lord grant you pardon, forgiveness, and remission of all your sins.

G **Amen.**

OR

L Almighty God, our heavenly Father,

G **we have sinned against you**
   in our thoughts,
   in our words,
   in our deeds,
   and in all that we have not done.
Forgive us in the name of our Lord Jesus Christ.
Deliver and restore us,
   that we may rest in peace.

L By the mercy of God we are redeemed by Jesus Christ,
   and in him we are forgiven.
Let us rest in his peace until the rising of the sun
   when we shall serve him in newness of life.

G **Amen.**

REMAIN SEATED

PSALM

One or more psalms are sung or said. Psalm 91 is usually first. See pages 61-69.

PSALM 91

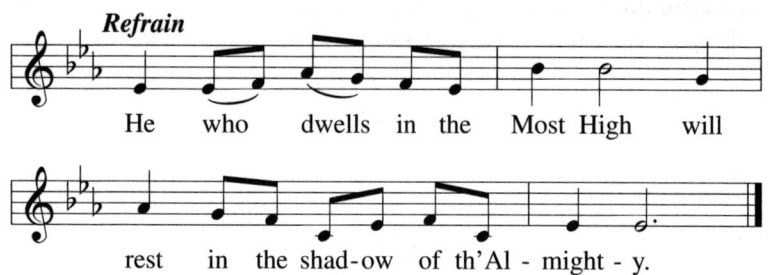

He who dwells in the shelter of the / Most High
 will rest in the shadow of the Al- / mighty.
  I will say / of the LORD,
   "He is my refuge and my fortress, my God, in / whom I trust."

Surely he will save you from the / fowler's snare
 and from the deadly / pestilence.
  He will cover you with his feathers, and under his wings you will find / refuge;
   his faithfulness will be your shield and / rampart.

Refrain

You will not fear the terror of night, nor the arrow that / flies by day,
 nor the pestilence that stalks in the darkness, nor the plague that destroys at / midday.
  A thousand may fall at your side, ten thousand at / your right hand,
   but it will not come / near you.

Refrain

If you make the Most High your dwelling—even the LORD, who is my / refuge—
 then no harm will befall you, no disaster will come / near your tent.
  For he will command his angels concerning you to guard you in / all your ways;
   they will lift you up in their hands, so that you will not strike your foot
    a- / gainst a stone.

**Glory be to the Father and / to the Son
  and to the Holy / Spirit,
    as it was in the be- / ginning,
      is now, and will be forever. / Amen.**

Refrain

Silence for meditation

|L| Lord God, our refuge and fortress, your faithfulness has protected us through this day. Now send your holy angels to guard us from danger through this night. Give us peaceful rest, free from fear, that we may wake refreshed to serve you, through Jesus Christ, your Son, our Lord.

|G| Amen.

LESSON

One or more of the following or other lessons are read.

The Spirit of the Sovereign LORD is on me, because the LORD has anointed me to preach good news to the poor. He has sent me to bind up the brokenhearted, to proclaim freedom for the captives and release from darkness for the prisoners, to proclaim the year of the LORD's favor and the day of vengeance of our God, to comfort all who mourn, and provide for those who grieve in Zion—to bestow on them a crown of beauty instead of ashes, the oil of gladness instead of mourning, and a garment of praise instead of a spirit of despair. They will be called oaks of righteousness, a planting of the LORD for the display of his splendor (Isaiah 61:1-3).

Although our sins testify against us, O LORD, do something for the sake of your name. For our backsliding is great; we have sinned against you. O Hope of Israel, its Savior in times of distress, why are you like a stranger in the land, like a traveler who stays only a night? Why are you like a man taken by surprise, like a warrior powerless to save? You are among us, O LORD, and we bear your name; do not forsake us! (Jeremiah 14:7-9).

Come to me, all you who are weary and burdened, and I will give you rest. Take my yoke upon you and learn from me, for I am gentle and humble in heart, and you will find rest for your souls. For my yoke is easy and my burden is light (Matthew 11:28-30).

Peace I leave with you; my peace I give you. I do not give to you as the world gives. Do not let your hearts be troubled and do not be afraid (John 14:27).

For I am convinced that neither death nor life, neither angels nor demons, neither the present nor the future, nor any powers, neither height nor depth, nor anything else in all creation, will be able to separate us from the love of God that is in Christ Jesus our Lord (Romans 8:38,39).

PRAYER AT THE CLOSE OF DAY II

May the God of peace, who through the blood of the eternal covenant brought back from the dead our Lord Jesus, that great Shepherd of the sheep, equip you with everything good for doing his will, and may he work in us what is pleasing to him, through Jesus Christ, to whom be glory for ever and ever. Amen (Hebrews 13:20,21).

Humble yourselves, therefore, under God's mighty hand, that he may lift you up in due time. Cast all your anxiety on him because he cares for you. Be self-controlled and alert. Your enemy the devil prowls around like a roaring lion looking for someone to devour. Resist him, standing firm in the faith, because you know that your brothers throughout the world are undergoing the same kind of sufferings (1 Peter 5:6-9).

The following response is sung or said.

L In - to your hands I com-mend my spir - it. G In - to your hands I com-mend my spir - it. L You have re-deemed me, O Lord, God of truth. G In - to your hands I com-mend my spir - it. L Glo - ry to the Fa - ther and to the Son (✠) and to the Ho - ly Spir - it. G In - to your hands I com - mend my spir - it.

54

PRAYER AT THE CLOSE OF DAY II

HYMN

PRAYER

The following are sung or said.

L Hear my prayer, O Lord. G Listen to my cry.
L Keep me as the apple of your eye. G Hide me in the shadow of your wings. L In righteousness I shall see you. G When I awake, your presence will give me joy.

One or more of the following prayers are sung or said.

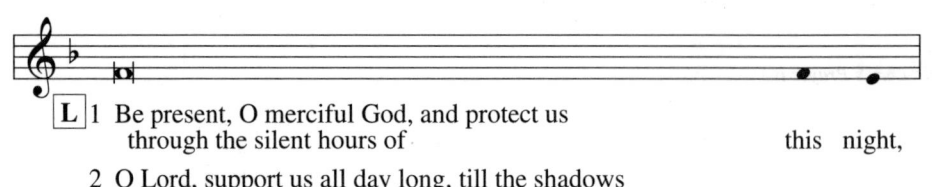

L 1 Be present, O merciful God, and protect us
through the silent hours of this night,

2 O Lord, support us all day long, till the shadows
lengthen and the evening comes and the busy world is
hushed and the fever of life is over and our work is done.

3 O God our Father, by your mercy and might, the world turns
safely into darkness and returns again to light. We place into
your hands our unfinished tasks, our unsolved problems, and
our unfulfilled hopes, knowing that only what you bless will pros - per.

4 Keep watch, dear Lord, with those who watch or work or weep
this night, and give your angels charge over those who sleep.

5 Look down, O Lord, from your heavenly throne,
and illuminate this night with your celestial bright-ness,

For Saturday

6 We give you thanks, O God, for revealing your
Son, Jesus Christ, to us by the light of his resur - rec - tion.

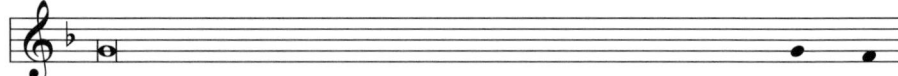

1 so that we who are wearied by the changes and chances
of this fleeting world may rest in your eternal change - less - ness,

2 Then in your mercy, grant us a safe
lodging and a holy rest and peace at the last,

3 To your great love and protection, we commit each other and
all those we love, knowing that you alone are our sure de - fen - der,

4 Tend the sick, give rest to the weary, pity the afflicted,
soothe the suffering, bless the dying—and all for your love's sake,

5 that by night as by day your people may glorify your hol - y name,

For Saturday

6 Grant that as we sing your glory at the close of this day, our
joy may abound in the morning as we celebrate the Paschal mys - tery,

Each prayer concludes:

LORD'S PRAYER

The Lord's Prayer is said, sung on a single tone, or sung as follows:

Our Father in heaven,	OR	Our Father, who art in heaven,

G Our Father in heaven,　　　　OR　　　Our Father, who art in heaven,
    hallowed be your name,　　　　　　　　hallowed be thy name,
    your kingdom come,　　　　　　　　　　thy kingdom come,
    your will be done　　　　　　　　　　　thy will be done
        on earth as in heaven.　　　　　　　　　on earth as it is in heaven.
Give us today our daily bread.　　　　Give us this day our daily bread;
Forgive us our sins,　　　　　　　　　and forgive us our trespasses,
    as we forgive those　　　　　　　　　　as we forgive those
    who sin against us.　　　　　　　　　　who trespass against us;
Lead us not into temptation,　　　　　and lead us not into temptation,
but deliver us from evil.　　　　　　　but deliver us from evil.
For the kingdom, the power,　　　　　For thine is the kingdom
    and the glory are yours　　　　　　　　and the power and the glory
    now and forever. Amen.　　　　　　　　forever and ever. Amen.

HYMN

GOSPEL CANTICLE

The following is sung or said.

L Guide us waking, O Lord, G and guard us sleeping; L that awake we may watch with Christ G and asleep we may rest in peace.

Song of Simeon

G In peace, Lord, in peace you let your servant now depart according to your word. For my eyes have seen your salvation, which you have prepared for ev-'ry people, a light to lighten the Gentiles and the glory of your people Israel. In peace, in peace.

BLESSING

L The almighty and merciful Lord—the Father, the Son, ✠ and the Holy Spirit—bless us and keep us.

G Amen.

INDEX FOR PSALM USE

Christian Worship: New Service Settings includes several new psalm settings. While these psalms are selected for use in Compline, some may also serve well in other services, especially evening services. The following chart shows additional days or occasions when these psalms may be used. Psalms appointed for the *Christian Worship* three-year lectionary are in regular type. Additional suggestions are in italic.

Psalm 4 ....*Lent 2C, Pentecost 2A*

Psalm 23 ....Easter 4ABC, Pentecost 9B, Pentecost 21A, *Christian Funeral*

Psalm 27 ....Epiphany 3A (verses 1-9), *Lent 4B* (verses 1-6 or 7-14*), Good Friday Tenebrae, Pentecost 9C*, Pentecost 18A (verses 1-9), Pentecost 20C, *Christian Funeral*

Psalm 31 ....*Lent 6ABC, Pentecost 2A,* Pentecost 5A, Pentecost 18B, Saint Stephen

Psalm 34 ....Pentecost 11C, Pentecost 12B, Pentecost 14A, *Pentecost 23C,* All Saints' Day

Psalm 91 ....Lent 1C, *Pentecost 5A,* Saint Michael and All Angels, *Time of Crisis*

Psalm 121 ....Lent 2A, *Pentecost 6B,* Pentecost 15A, Pentecost 22C, Saint Bartholomew, *Christian Funeral*

Psalm 130 ....Advent 2A, Advent 3C, Epiphany 7B, *Ash Wednesday,* Lent 1A, The Holy Innocents, *Christian Funeral, Corporate Confession*

Psalm 134 ....Pentecost 13A, *Church Dedication*

Psalm 4

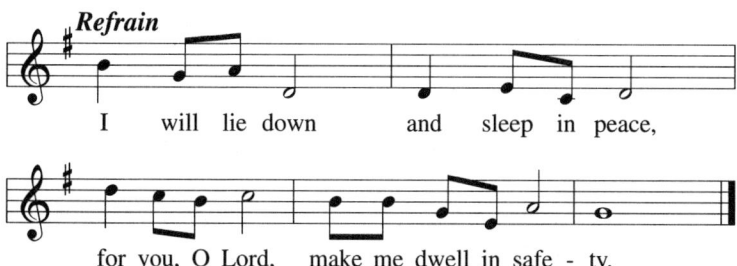

Answer me when I call to you, O my / righteous God.
  Give me relief from my distress; be merciful to me and / hear my prayer.
    How long, O men, will you turn my glory / into shame?
      How long will you love delusions and / seek false gods?

Know that the LORD has set apart the godly / for himself;
  the LORD will hear when I / call to him.
    In your anger / do not sin;
      when you are on your beds, search your hearts and be / silent.

Refrain

Offer right sacri- / fices
  and trust / in the LORD.
    Many are asking, "Who can show us / any good?"
      Let the light of your face shine upon us, / O LORD.

You have filled my heart with / greater joy
  than when their grain and new / wine abound.
    I will lie down and / sleep in peace,
      for you alone, O LORD, make me dwell in / safety.

Refrain

Glory be to the Father and / to the Son
  and to the Holy / Spirit,
    as it was in the be- / ginning,
      is now, and will be forever. / Amen.

Refrain

Psalm Prayer on page 70.

Psalm 23

The LORD is my / shepherd,
   I shall not / be in want.
      He makes me lie down in green / pastures,
         he leads me beside quiet / waters,

he re- / stores my soul.
   He guides me in paths of righteousness for his / name's sake.
      Even though I walk through the valley of the shadow of death,
      I will fear no evil, for you are / with me;
         your rod and your staff, they / comfort me.

Refrain

You prepare a table before me in the presence of my / enemies.
   You anoint my head with oil; my cup / overflows.
      Surely goodness and love will follow me all the days / of my life,
         and I will dwell in the house of the LORD for- / ever.

Glory be to the Father and / to the Son
   and to the Holy / Spirit,
      as it was in the be- / ginning,
      is now, and will be forever. / Amen.

Refrain

Psalm Prayer on page 70.

Psalm 27

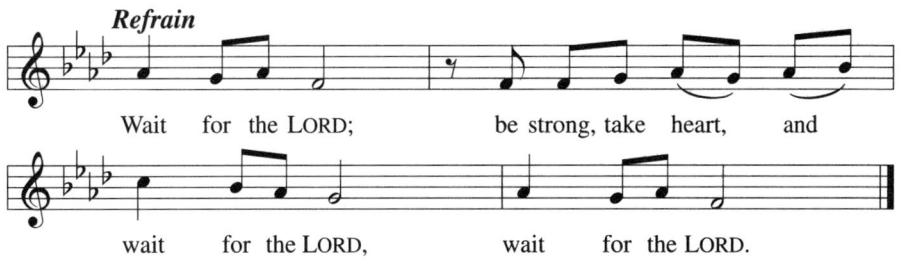

The LORD is my light and my salvation—whom / shall I fear?
    The LORD is the stronghold of my life—of whom shall I / be afraid?
        When evil men advance against me to de- / vour my flesh,
            when my enemies and my foes attack me, they will stum- / ble and fall.

One thing I ask of the LORD, this is / what I seek:
    that I may dwell in the house of the LORD all the days of my life, to gaze
    upon the beauty of the LORD and to seek him in his / temple.
        For in the day of trouble he will keep me safe in his / dwelling;
        he will hide me in the shelter of his tabernacle
            and set me high up- / on a rock.

Refrain

Hear my voice when I / call, O LORD;
    be merciful to me and / answer me.
        My heart says of you, / "Seek his face!"
            Your face, LORD, / I will seek.

Do not hide your / face from me,
    do not turn your servant away in / anger;
        you have been my / helper.
            Do not reject me or forsake me, O God my / Savior.

Refrain

I am still confi- / dent of this:
    I will see the goodness of the LORD in the land of the / living.
        Wait / for the LORD;
            be strong and take heart and wait / for the LORD.

Glory be to the Father and / to the Son
    and to the Holy / Spirit,
        as it was in the be- / ginning,
            is now, and will be forever. / Amen.

Refrain

Psalm Prayer on page 70.

Psalm 31

Refrain: I trust in you, O LORD; I say, "You are my God."

Psalm tone

In you, O LORD, I have taken refuge; let me never be / put to shame;
   deliver me in your / righteousness.
      Turn your ear to me, come quickly to my / rescue;
         be my rock of refuge, a strong fortress to / save me.

Since you are my rock and my / fortress,
   for the sake of your name lead and / guide me.
      Free me from the trap that is / set for me,
         for you are my / refuge.

Refrain

Into your hands I commit my / spirit;
   redeem me, O LORD, the / God of truth.
      I hate those who cling to worthless / idols;
         I trust / in the LORD.

I will be glad and rejoice / in your love,
   for you saw my affliction and knew the anguish / of my soul.
      You have not handed me over to the / enemy
         but have set my feet in a / spacious place.

Refrain

Be merciful to me, O LORD, for I am / in distress;
   my eyes grow weak with sorrow, my soul and my body / with grief.
      My life is consumed by anguish and my years by / groaning;
         my strength fails because of my affliction, and my / bones grow weak.

But I trust in / you, O LORD;
   I say, "You / are my God."
      My times are / in your hands;
         deliver me from my enemies and from those who pur- / sue me.

Refrain

Love the LORD, / all his saints!
   The LORD preserves the faithful, but the proud he pays / back in full.
      Be strong / and take heart,
         all you who hope / in the LORD.

Glory be to the Father and / to the Son
   and to the Holy / Spirit,
      as it was in the be- / ginning,
         is now, and will be forever. / Amen.

Refrain

Psalm Prayer on page 70.

Psalm 34

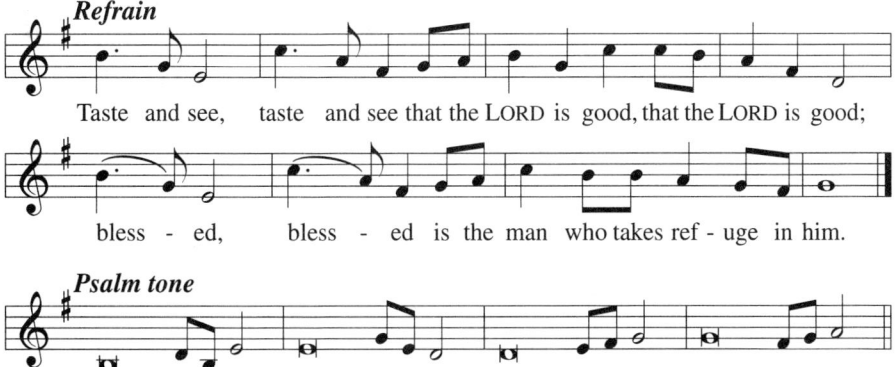

I will extol the LORD at / all times;
    his praise will always be / on my lips.
        My soul will boast / in the LORD;
            let the afflicted hear / and rejoice.

Glorify the / LORD with me;
    let us exalt his name to- / gether.
        I sought the LORD, and he / answered me;
            he delivered me from / all my fears.

Refrain

Those who look to him are / radiant;
    their faces are never covered / with shame.
        This poor man called, and the LORD / heard him;
            he saved him out of all his / troubles.

The angel of the LORD encamps around those who / fear him,
    and he de- / livers them.
        Taste and see that the / LORD is good;
            blessed is the man who takes ref- / uge in him.

Refrain

Fear the LORD, / you his saints,
    for those who fear him lack / nothing.
        The lions may grow weak and / hungry,
            but those who seek the LORD lack / no good thing.

Glory be to the Father and / to the Son
    and to the Holy / Spirit,
        as it was in the be- / ginning,
            is now, and will be forever. / Amen.

Refrain

Psalm Prayer on page 70.

Psalm 91

Because you are my help, I sing in the shadow of your wings.

He who dwells in the shelter of the / Most High
> will rest in the shadow of the Al- / mighty.
>> I will say / of the LORD,
>>> "He is my refuge and my fortress, my God, in / whom I trust."

Surely he will save you from the / fowler's snare
> and from the deadly / pestilence.
>> He will cover you with his feathers,
>> and under his wings you will find / refuge;
>>> his faithfulness will be your shield and / rampart.

Refrain

You will not fear the terror of night, nor the arrow that / flies by day,
> nor the pestilence that stalks in the darkness,
> nor the plague that destroys at / midday.
>> A thousand may fall at your side, ten thousand at / your right hand,
>> but it will not come / near you.

Refrain

If you make the Most High your dwelling—even the LORD,
who is my / refuge—
> then no harm will befall you, no disaster will come / near your tent.
>> For he will command his angels concerning you
>> to guard you in / all your ways;
>>> they will lift you up in their hands,
>>> so that you will not strike your foot a- / gainst a stone.

Glory be to the Father and / to the Son
> **and to the Holy / Spirit,**
>> **as it was in the be- / ginning,**
>>> **is now, and will be forever. / Amen.**

Refrain

Psalm Prayer on page 71.

Psalm 121

I lift up my eyes / to the hills—
    where does / my help come from?
        My help comes / from the LORD,
            the Maker of heav- / en and earth.

He will not let your / foot slip—
    he who watches over you / will not slumber;
        indeed, he who watches over / Israel
            will neither slum- / ber nor sleep.

Refrain

The LORD watches / over you—
    the LORD is your shade at / your right hand;
        the sun will not harm / you by day,
            nor the / moon by night.

The LORD will keep you / from all harm—
    he will watch o- / ver your life;
        the LORD will watch over your coming and / going
            both now and for- / evermore.

Refrain

Glory be to the Father and / to the Son
    and to the / Holy Spirit,
        as it was in the be- / ginning,
            is now, and will be forev- / er. Amen.

Refrain

Psalm Prayer on page 71.

Psalm 130

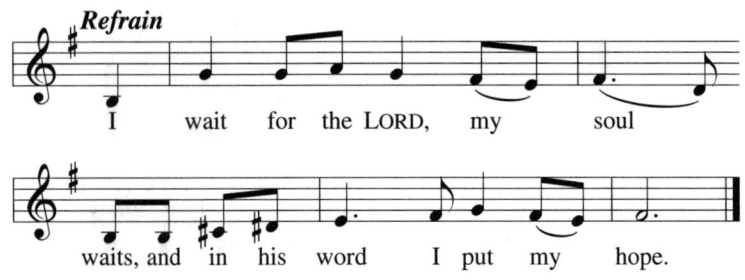

Out / of the depths
   I cry to / you, O LORD;
      O Lord, / hear my voice.
         Let your ears be attentive to my cry for / mercy.

If you, O LORD, kept a rec- / ord of sins,
   O Lord, / who could stand?
      But with you there is for- / giveness;
         therefore / you are feared.

Refrain

I wait for the LORD, my / soul waits,
   and in his word I / put my hope.
      My soul waits for the Lord more than watchmen wait for the / morning,
         more than watchmen wait for the / morning.

O Israel, put your hope / in the LORD,
   for with the LORD is unfailing love and with him is full re- / demption.
      He himself will redeem / Israel
         from / all their sins.

Refrain

**Glory be to the Father and / to the Son
   and to the Holy / Spirit,
      as it was in the be- / ginning,
         is now, and will be forever. / Amen.**

Refrain

Psalm Prayer on page 71.

Psalm 134

Praise the Lord.

All you servants of the LORD who
   minister by / night in the
     house of the LORD.

Refrain

Lift up your hands in the
   sanctu- / ary and
     praise the LORD.

Refrain

May the LORD, the Maker of
   heaven and earth, / bless you from
     Zion.

Refrain

Glory be to the
   Father and to the Son and to / the Holy
     Spirit,

Refrain

as it was in the be-
   ginning, is now, and will be for- / ever. A-
     men.

Refrain

Psalm Prayer on page 71.

PSALM PRAYERS

Psalm 4

Lord, you consoled your Son in his anguish and released him from the darkness of the grave. Turn your face toward us, that we may sleep in peace and wake to live in your light, through Jesus Christ, your Son, our Lord.

Psalm 23

Lord Jesus Christ, Shepherd of the Church, in the waters of Baptism you have given us new life and at your table you nourish us with the food of salvation. Lead us along safe paths through the darkness of this world, dispel the terrors of death, and bring us at last to your house, where you dwell with the Father and the Holy Spirit, one God, now and forever.

Psalm 27

Gracious Father, you have been the light and salvation of your people in every age. Bring us, we pray, through the troubles of this present life, that we may see your goodness in eternity, through your Son, Jesus Christ our Lord.

Psalm 31

God, our Rock and Fortress, protect your people who confess your name, and strengthen the hearts of those who trust your mercy, that they may proclaim your goodness and praise you for your unfailing love, through your Son, Jesus Christ our Lord.

Psalm 34

Dearest Lord, helper of the weary and the brokenhearted, we have tasted and seen that you are good and ready to help in time of trouble. Calm our minds with peace, and make us radiant with joy, through your Son, Jesus Christ our Lord.

Psalm 91

Lord God, our refuge and fortress, your faithfulness has protected us through this day. Now send your holy angels to guard us from danger through this night. Give us peaceful rest, free from fear, that we may wake refreshed to serve you, through Jesus Christ, your Son, our Lord.

Psalm 121

Lord God, you never slumber nor sleep, but your eyes are always open to our needs. Watch over our welfare on this perilous journey, shade us from the dangers that surround us, and keep us safe from harm, through Jesus Christ, your Son, our Lord.

Psalm 130

God of might and compassion, open your ears to the prayers of your people who wait for you. Do not leave us in the depths of our sins, but listen to your Church pleading for the fullness of your redemption, through Jesus Christ our Lord.

Psalm 134

Lord Jesus, where two or three gather in your name, you promised to be with them and share their fellowship. Look on us, your family, and graciously bless us with unity and harmony, for you live and reign with the Father and the Holy Spirit, one God, now and forever.

ACKNOWLEDGEMENTS

All Scripture quotations, unless otherwise indicated, are taken from the HOLY BIBLE, NEW INTERNATIONAL VERSION®. NIV®. Copyright © 1973, 1978, 1984 by International Bible Society. Used by permission of Zondervan Publishing House. All rights reserved.

The English translation of the Nicene Creed prepared by the English Language Liturgical Consultation (ELLC), 1988, altered.

The following authors, composers, and sources are acknowledged.

The Common Service

Texts revised from *The Lutheran Hymnal,* 1941.
Music by Kermit Moldenhauer. © 2002 Northwestern Publishing House.

Morning Praise

Texts revised from *The Lutheran Hymnal,* 1941.

"Blessing,"
"Song of Zechariah,"
"Come, Oh, Come, Let Us Sing to the Lord,"
"Prayer for Grace,"
Prayer Response,
"You Are God; We Praise You" ....Marty Haugen. Text, Tune, Setting: © 1995, 1996 by GIA Publications, Inc. 7404 So. Mason Ave., Chicago, IL 60638. International copyright secured. All rights reserved.

"Lord, Have Mercy"..Kermit Moldenhauer. Tune, Setting: © 2002 Northwestern Publishing House.

Opening Sentences...Marty Haugen and Kermit Moldenhauer. Text, Tune, Setting: © 1995, 1996 by GIA Publications, Inc. 7404 So. Mason Ave., Chicago, IL 60638. International copyright secured. All rights reserved. And © 2002 Northwestern Publishing House.

Psalm 63..Marty Haugen. Text for verses: © 1936, 1986, 1993 The Grail, England, GIA Publications, Inc. exclusive North American agent. Text for refrain, Tune, Setting: © 1995, 1996 by GIA Publications, Inc. 7404 So. Mason Ave., Chicago, IL 60638. International copyright secured. All rights reserved.

Compline I

Text for "Confession of Sins" reprinted from *Lutheran Book of Worship, Ministers Desk Edition* © 1978 by permission of Augsburg Fortress.

Text for Prayers from *The Book of Common Prayer* (1979) of the Episcopal Church, USA.

Text for "Gospel Canticle" from *The Book of Common Prayer* (1979) of the Episcopal Church, USA.

"Evening Hymn" ....Setting: © 1969 Concordia Publishing House. Used by permission of CPH.

"Blessing,"
"Gospel Canticle,"
Lesson Response,
Opening Sentences,
Prayer Introduction,
Prayers,
"Psalm 91" ....Music by Kermit Moldenhauer. © 2002 Northwestern Publishing House.

Compline II

Text for "Confession of Sins" reprinted from *Lutheran Book of Worship, Ministers Desk Edition* © 1978 by permission of Augsburg Fortress.

Text for Prayers from *The Book of Common Prayer* (1979) of the Episcopal Church, USA.

Text for "Gospel Canticle" from *The Book of Common Prayer* (1979) of the Episcopal Church, USA.

ACKNOWLEDGEMENTS

"Evening Hymn" .... Setting: © 1969 Concordia Publishing House. Used by permission of CPH.

"Gospel Canticle,"
Lesson Response,
"Lord's Prayer,"
Opening Sentences,
Prayer Introduction,
Prayers,
"Psalm 91" .... Music by Dale Witte. © 2002 Northwestern Publishing House.

Psalms

Music by Dale Witte. Tunes and Settings: © 2002 Northwestern Publishing House.

Psalm Prayers

Psalms 4, 91 .... © 2002 Northwestern Publishing House.

Psalms 23, 27, 31, 34, 121 .... © 1993 Northwestern Publishing House.

Psalms 130, 134 .... Adapted and reprinted from *Lutheran Book of Worship: Minister's Desk Edition,* © 1978, by permission of Augsburg Fortress.

ISBN 0-8100-1401-7

03N3024

The PASSION HISTORY

ACCORDING TO
THE FOUR GOSPELS

THE PASSION HISTORY
ACCORDING TO THE FOUR GOSPELS

Compiled from the

NEW INTERNATIONAL VERSION

of the New Testament

Arranged by

CLAYTON E. KRUG

Copyright 1975

by

NORTHWESTERN PUBLISHING HOUSE

Milwaukee, Wisconsin

Second Edition 1981

Printed with permission of the New York Bible Society International
ISBN 0-8100-0047-4